Coming Home With

The sovereignty of Love

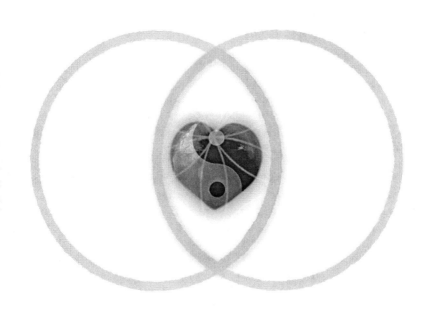

Alaya Denoyelles

◊ Vesica Publishing

◊ Vᴇsɪᴄᴀ Pᴜʙʟɪsʜɪɴɢ

Vesica Publishing
Kauai, Hawaii
Copyright ©2012, Alaya DeNoyelles. All rights reserved.

Paperback ISBN: 978-0-9848213-0-3
Hard Cover ISBN: 978-0-9848213-1-0
Library of Congress Control Number: 2012931661
Copyright No. TXul-759-138

Interior design: J. L. Saloff
Cover design: Manjari Graphics
Typography: Constantia, Savoye
Cover Photo of author, Paddy Kean and Spencer McDonald,
    www.mcdonaldkeanphotography.com

All images used with permission. See: End Notes for copyright
information.

v. 1.02
First Edition, March 2012
Printed on acid-free paper.

This book is lovingly dedicated to Kauai,
The magical garden island of Hawaii.

My prayer is that you experience in your life the
qualities that I've received from her:
Unfathomable love, harmony and peace.

Contents

Part Three: Harmonizing

Introduction

A *Akahai*——to be kind

L *Lokahi*——to be harmonious

O *Olu'olu*——to be agreeable

H *Ha'aha'a*——to be humble

A *Ahonui*——to be patient

The Bowl of Light

Each child is born with a perfect bowl of light. This bowl represents her true identity, a vessel of shining light. If she is taught to love and respect her light, then she will grow in strength and health and she can do anything – swim with the shark, fly with the birds, know and understand all things. If, however, she judges her experience of life as bad and becomes fearful, ashamed, or resentful, she drops a stone into her bowl of light and it blocks some of the light. The stone and the light cannot hold the same space. If she continues to put stones in the bowl, it will eventually be full of stones, the light will go out, and she will become a stone. A stone does not grow, nor does it move. If at any time she tires of being a stone, all she needs to do is turn the bowl upside down and the stones will fall out, and the light will grow bright once more.

*I*n this Hawaiian story, the bowl of light represents our true essence: pure light, pure love. When we are conscious and respectful of this light, we are living in our highest state of freedom, our sovereignty.

The stones in the bowl represent the pain and suffering that we cause ourselves by resisting life instead of trusting it, and by not accepting others or ourselves as we are.

If we fill our bowl of light with stones, we lose connection with our essence and feel separate from the source of love and light.

It would be nice if we could just dump our stones out and start over again. The reality is that all of our experiences, both painful and pleasurable, will always be part of who we are. It's not possible to deny or eliminate them. What we can do is return the light to our bowl so that the memories of our wounds no longer affect us negatively. We can turn our stones into crystals. We polish them with our loving presence. This is the alchemy that transforms our experiences of pain and suffering into a treasure chest of pristine, multi-faceted jewels. Our bowl of light is now full of shimmering, sparkling crystals, representing a richly lived life.

The Harmonizing practice presented in this book is a method of tending our stones and restoring the light in our bowl.

Introduction

I live on the tropical island of Kauai, and am pro-
foundly influenced daily by its magnificent, soft,
nurturing qualities that embrace my being on every
level. Kauai is the oldest of the Hawaiian islands, which
comprise the most remote and isolated land mass on the
planet.

The *aloha spirit* is well known for its warmhearted,
welcoming attitude. *Aloha* means much more than hello
or goodbye; it is a cultural protocol, a way of life. *Aloha*
is a compound word composed of *alo*, meaning presence, sharing or facing, and *ha*, meaning breath, or the
essence of life. *Aloha* symbolically means to share breath
and to be present with the essence of life, which is love.
When we think or say the word *aloha*, we generate loving
vibration and attune ourselves to the Divine or Spiritual
Power, what Hawaiians call *mana*.

Traditionally, Hawaiians know that honoring, loving,
respecting, and being *pono* (correct) in all relationships

is vital to a harmonious life. When there is conflict, injustice or disharmony amongst the family, they can restore harmony using a process called Ho'oponopono, an ancient healing art of conflict resolution. The purpose of Ho'oponopono is to return the *aloha* (the breath of life) back into the family.

The Harmonizing practice offered in this book is based on Ho'oponopono. It is a way to restore our Bowl of Light, to harmonize our stones of wounds and pain, and bring back the light of *aloha*, our essence of love.

This work has been inspired by the energy, the mana (spiritual power) of the aina (environment) that I experience here on Kauai, primarily from the top of a mountain that overlooks her lush tropical forests, fertile valleys, and the vast expanse of the Pacific Ocean. I have been the conduit for this work; however, its creator is this island. My prayer is that I've honored her magnificence and that her *mana* is felt when you read this book and experience the practices given.

The phrase '*sovereignty of love*' came to me one day as I was coming down this mountain where I often hike and meditate. Not knowing how to spell *sovereignty*, let alone define it, I simply trusted the message, then went home and researched its meaning. Webster loosely defines sovereignty as *'our highest autonomous state.'* I learned that sovereignty means freedom and empowerment, giving rise to the deeply satisfying, peaceful feeling of wholeness, of home within myself. Ultimately, I've come to know it as *self-love*.

This is how this book was written. During my hike up *Nounou* (the Sleeping Giant), or when I was sitting up on top meditating, inspirations would come. I would pick up a flower or twig on the trail and infuse it with my inspiration so that I could later remember the essence of the message. I would then hike down the mountain with my hands, my pockets, my bra full of strawberry guava, blossoms, pinecones, leaves, or rocks. Once home I laid them out on my desk and began typing up the inspirations they represented. I would then research the scientific or spiritual teachings that seemed related to the inspiration I received on my hike. Captivated with old and new scientific research, I devoured everything I could find on the hologram theory, vibration, consciousness, the heart, and sacred geometry. Gregg Braden, Bruce Lipton, Dr. Masaru Emoto, and Nassim Haramein, amongst others, became my heroes. It was like putting together a jigsaw puzzle, as all the pieces seemed to fit together perfectly. Over the course of three years, the weaving of these inspirations and discoveries became this book.

Invariably, each inspiration became a lesson presented to me by the circumstances of my life. As each lesson came, I was willing to experience it, live it, and embody it in order to understand the true meaning of the message. Often this was a very painful process as I dealt with intense relationship and health struggles, eventually learning to trust and welcome the gifts embedded in the suffering.

I found that by using the process of Ho'oponopono when challenges came up in my life, I was able to experience my pain, accept it, take responsibility for it, offer it my love, and see it dissolve back into peace. Doing this process over time, I found myself more and more in a blissful state that took me to a peace beyond anything I'd ever experienced. Miraculously, I watched as my stones transformed into crystals. The process I had discovered became an integral part of my acupuncture and healing practice. I was excited to witness the transformative power of the practice with my clients and in workshops.

Introduction

This book is written in three parts. Part One discusses the universal principles of Love, Vibration, and Duality. Part Two delivers the fundamental elements necessary to embody the Harmonizing Practice given in Part Three. These elements are Ho'oponopono, Consciousness, Self-Responsibility, Holographic Universe, the Heart, and Sacred Geometry.

Our sense of separation from our essence, which is love, is the cause of our suffering. This book is about reuniting our consciousness with love, restoring our shining bowl of light.

Part One

The Universal Principles

Sitting alone in your room, be loving. Radiate love. Fill the whole room with your love energy, as if you are in an ocean of love. Create vibrations of love energy around you... ~ Osho

A Creation Metaphor

In the beginning there was unlimited, pure vibration. In this formless, timeless, neutral expanse, a portal appeared, which was the womb that gave creation a place from which to be birthed. This womb carried a specific vibrational frequency called Love. Love became the matrix, the fabric, the embrace that would hold all of creation. In order for love to experience itself, it gave birth to a pair of soul mates who were opposites of one another. This was Duality.

Duality, the realm of polarity in which we find ourselves, is the opportunity to physically and emotionally experience the movement of love.

Vibration is the pulse of the universe, Love is the source of creation, and Duality is the venue in which existence plays itself out.

Chapter One

Love

Everything starts with love, remember; love is the ulti-
mate law . . . the world is only a school to learn the art
of love. ~ Osho

The Pulse of the Universe

*L*ove is the vibrational frequency of the universe, the holographic web that connects all of creation.

Love is the generating pulse, the vibrational hum, the rhythm of the universe. It is the foundation for all existence. Everything manifest is birthed upon the waves of this frequency, so it is this fabric of love that binds us together, individually as well as collectively.

This frequency we call Love is our soul's essence, our Divinity within, our life force, our breath.

The original frequency of love has no concept of separation or duality, right or wrong, yes or no. It is a neutral vibration — unconditionally allowing and embracing everything.

Our relationship with our essence (love) has been compromised due to the emotional chaos and deep grief we have experienced as humans. We suffer under the illusion of isolation, of separateness from love, our source.

All our lives, we have sought to experience this love, which is the truth of our nature. We reach out into the world hoping to find it in another person, in security, possessions, accomplishments, power, and wealth. It may be the primary underlying motivation of our life as humans to feel this vibration of love pulsing through us, alleviating our suffering and the emptiness we feel inside.

We are accustomed to thinking of love as something we share with another, but the oneness that we truly seek is the communion with our own Essence, our God or Goddess within.

This inner communion is the seed, the foundation, and the source of all other authentic connection with something or someone outside of ourselves. The degree to which we cultivate love within ourselves determines the degree to which we are available for communion with others, and with all of life.

Physics of Love

Loosely defined, Physics is the scientific study of energy, matter, and motion, and the way they relate to each other.

In the context of this work, Physics explains how the energy of our essence, our love, interacts through vibration with the various aspects of our consciousness.

Love

"The common connecting link between substance and energy is vibration. And the common vibratory phenomenon that connects vibration is sympathy. When two or more things possess the same chord of mass or chord of vibration (vibration signature) those things are then said to be in sympathy and associate sympathetically one to the other as though they were One thing. When one thing vibrates, the others vibrate in sympathy with it or we say they all vibrate as One. In real human terms, we call sympathy or sympathetic association—LOVE. This is the Law that binds molecules together. This is the Law that when broken causes chaos, discord and disruption. This is the Law that when adhered to brings peace, harmony and understanding into all life and all life's activities."

~ from 'The Physics of Love' by Dale Pond

When our consciousness is in sympathetic resonance (harmony) with our essence (love), we are in tune with the Universal Law that Love binds the universe together. When our consciousness is in discord, we are in chaos. Returning to sympathetic resonance with our essence is the purpose of this work.

In the chapters to follow, we will explore a process that guides us to return to our natural capacity to feel the elixir of love inside ourselves.

Summary

♡ Love is the vibrational frequency of the universe.

♡ Love is our soul's essence.

♡ We suffer because we feel separate from love.

Chapter Two

Vibration

Vibration is that same energy, same power, ye call God.

~ Edgar Cayce

Everything is Vibration

*T*he vast ocean of Love surrounds, embraces, connects, and weaves all of creation together; gently pulsing, dancing, undulating: a magnificent symphony of living molecules.

Nothing is static. Everything in our universe (seen and unseen) is a vibrating kaleidoscope of atoms and subatomic particles. This includes all thoughts, words and emotions. Thoughts emit vibrational frequencies that resonate out from our body. Individually, we each have a unique and constantly changing array of vibrational frequencies that are distinctly our own. These unique vibrational signatures manifest the current state of our individual reality.

We choose in every moment, consciously or unconsciously, via what we are thinking and feeling, what vibratory frequency we will experience in our body, and thus create in our life.

Vibration

Everything vibrates at a certain rate, a specific frequency. An example of a vibrating material object is a piece of paper. When you pick it up and look at it, it appears to be a solid object. If you were to tear off a small piece of the corner and place it under a microscope, you would see it transform into a moving object. The movement that you see is millions of individual molecules which make up the piece of paper. Everything in our world that you can sense with the five basic human senses is made up of these tiny wonders. Actually billions and trillions of them. If you isolate one of these molecules, you will also see movement. The atoms that make up the molecule are dancing. Broken down and analyzed further, you will see an electron constantly orbiting around a proton. This is what creates the vibratory pattern, also known as energy.

Thought is one of the most powerful forms of vibration. When you are thinking a thought you are emitting a specific frequency, sending it out to the universe and therefore calling matching resonance back to you.

Sympathetic Resonance

When two objects of similar frequency are brought near each other, they have an effect on each other. Sympathetic resonance is the unison that occurs when neighboring vibrations of similar frequency respond to one another. They are then said to be in sympathy. This happens with individuals, musical instruments, nature; any two or more vibrating masses of atoms and molecules.

For an illustration of sympathetic resonance, strike a tuning fork and hold it in close proximity to another fork tuned to the same note. Within seconds, the second fork will also begin to vibrate.

This happens because the energy waves (sound waves) from the fork that was struck traveled through the air and activated the second fork. The second fork came into sympathetic resonance with the first.

If you have ever been in the presence of a joyous infant or young child and immediately felt a whelming of love arise within you, you have come into the sympathetic resonance of love with them. Similar resonance happens when you are in the vibrational field of an enlightened master or powerfully peaceful person. This is also a common experience upon entering certain

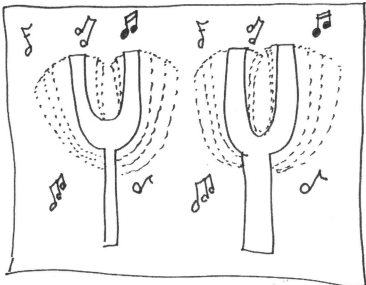

Sympathetic Resonance

environments or structures. Walking in nature or into a cathedral or temple, we are spiritually nurtured as we come into sympathetic resonance with the environment, feeling its sacredness and harmony.

Law of Attraction

The Law of Attraction states that like attracts like.

The popular interpretation of this concept is that we attract to ourselves, from the world, whatever we focus upon. For example, if we focus on finding the loving partner or job that we want, we will attract it to us. Or if we focus on the negatives in life, we will actually get more of what we do not want.

In my view, this law does not mean that we attract anything from the world, but simply that we create an outer manifestation of what already exists within us. So we do not get what we want from the world; instead we project that which is within us out into the world, and this is perpetually mirrored back to us.

Here, what is being proposed is that the way to bring things into our lives is to first feel on a visceral level the vibration of what we desire to experience. As we feel this frequency within us, we then radiate it into our environment. If we desire peace, for example, we can practice feeling peace in our body, and this will radiate into all aspects of our life. This intention is a conscious choice we can make, and this book explores how it works.

Frequency of Water

Dr. Masaru Emoto is a visionary scientist who researches the crystalline structure of water. He studies the phenomenon that words and thoughts have specific vibrational signatures that greatly influence the molecular structure of water.

Dr. Emoto conducted an experiment with groups of people circled around containers of water. The individuals consciously sent a variety of thoughts, prayers and emotions into the water, which was then swiftly frozen and later observed for its molecular patterns.

They discovered that the crystalline structure of the frozen water reflected the vibrational energy that was sent to it. Negative energy or words like 'you fool' or 'I'm angry' destroyed the crystalline water clusters, and chaotic or non-cohesive shapes formed. Positive words like 'I love you' or 'I'm grateful' generated beautiful, precisely geometric, cohesive hexagonal crystals that looked like snowflakes.

Another experiment involved writing words on pieces of paper and adhering them to containers of water. Again the molecular structure of the water changed to reflect the energy of the written words.

Dr. Emoto found that two words used individually or combined had the strongest crystallizing effect on the water. Those words were *Love* and *Gratitude.*

Professor Konstantin Korotkov from the Russian Academy of Sciences has done similar research using Bio-electrography technology that measures changes in the water's frequency rather than particle structure. The frequency measurements taken on water samples showed that when thoughts of love, tenderness, concern and care were directed toward a flask of water, the electrical energy of the water increased. Negative thoughts of fear, aggression and hatred caused the energy to decline. In daily life this can be observed as increased or decreased vitality in our bodies.

Our Body's Water

Depending upon our age, our body is composed of 70-90% water. The molecular structure of this water is crucial to our health, as it makes up and nourishes every cell and organ.

Our Body is an oscillating crystalline structure of water. It is in a constant state of restructuring itself to resonate with our current emotional state, be it anger, joy, sadness, appreciation, stress or relaxation. The crystalline structure of the water in our body is like a tuning fork, always seeking to be in sympathetic resonance with the 'feeling' tuning fork of our beliefs, thoughts and emotions.

Some Tibetan doctors listen to the energy pulses in the wrists, which reflect the quality of *Qi* or life force in the patient, thereby assessing the frequency or resonance of water in the body. Often the doctors prescribe specific mantras or chants which will change the resonance and frequency of the body's water. This method of healing addresses the body's overall state of disharmony directly, not just the presenting symptom.

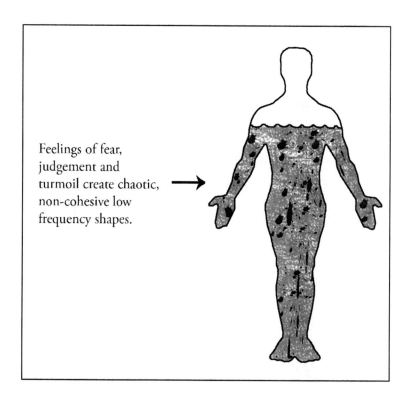

Feelings of fear, judgement and turmoil create chaotic, non-cohesive low frequency shapes.

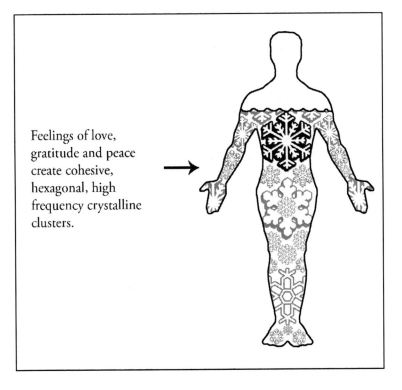

Feelings of love, gratitude and peace create cohesive, hexagonal, high frequency crystalline clusters.

Summary

♡ Everything is vibration, including thoughts, words and emotions.

♡ Our thoughts emit vibrational frequencies internally and externally.

♡ Our frequency attracts matching frequencies to itself.

♡ Our thoughts, feelings and emotions program our body.

Exercises

FEELING THE BODY'S ENERGY —
DISSONANCE AND RESONANCE

This exercise is for distinguishing the feelings of tension and relaxation (dissonance and resonance) in your body.

Begin by connecting with your breath.

Take a deep breath and hold it—tensing your whole body as tightly as possible.

Hold your breath and tightness for several seconds and then exhale forcibly.

Breathing normally, allow all the tension in your body to fully relax.

Do this several times to give you an exaggerated sense of the contrast between dissonance and resonance.

TONING — SOUNDING

Utilizing the built-in musical instrument of your voice box is a fantastic way to feel vibration in your body. Note that there is no right or wrong way to do this exercise.

Get into a comfortable position (sitting or standing) and take a few deep breaths to relax and center yourself.

Clear your throat. Close your eyes and begin to express whatever sounds come naturally out of your throat and mouth.

Experiment with the pitch, tone and various sounds playfully. Make some specific tones such as OM or HUE or sound the vowels: A, E, I, O, U or the notes: Do Re Me Fa So La Ti Do. Let your creativity guide you and flow through you. Feel the vibrations of different tones and pitches move within your body, and notice which feel in resonance or dissonance.

Chapter Three

Duality

Tao is one; then it divides itself into two,
yin and yang, darkness and light, life and death.
But the reality is One.
~ The Secret of the Golden Flower

*D*uality is the amphitheater in which the dance of the universe plays out. The principle of duality states that everything has an equal opposite. Without duality we would not have physical experience, no sun and moon, no male and female, no joy and sorrow, no discovery and loss, no rest and activity, no birth and death, no free choice.

Yin and Yang

The Yin-Yang symbol represents the ancient Chinese understanding of how creation expresses itself. The outer circle represents 'everything', while the interlocking black and white shapes within the circle represent the interaction of two energies, called 'yin' (black) and 'yang' (white).

This classic universal image of harmony represents the union of opposite polarities, the principle of sacred duality. There is no conflict here. The dark does not suppress the light, nor does the light stifle the dark. Entwined and interdependent, they spoon together to create a unified whole, always vibrating and moving, each containing the seed of the other.

Opposites are actually two extremes of the same thing, with many varying degrees between them. Heat and cold, light and dark, giving and receiving... though opposites, they dance on a continuum between the ends of the spectrum.

Various spiritual traditions instruct us to transcend duality in order to experience Oneness. But to fully embrace all of life, we must embrace contrast, as it is a governing principle of existence. To deny this spectrum of opposites is to deny a fully engaged life. It is not duality itself that causes us suffering; it is our inability to find emotional and mental harmony within the variety of contrasts that present themselves. In its balance and magnificence, duality provides us the opportunity to experience all the gifts of creation and choose how we relate to them.

Yin	Yang
Feminine	Masculine
Dark/Night	Light/Day
Negative	Positive
Moon	Sun
Fall/Winter	Spring/Summer
Valleys	Mountains
Being	Doing
Stillness	Motion
Silence	Sound
Right Brain	Left Brain
Subconscious Mind	Conscious Mind
Surrender	Control
Flow	Structure
Emotional	Mental
Internal	External
Downward	Upward
Rest	Work
Cold	Heat
Matter	Spirit
Hollow	Solid
Soft	Hard
Passive	Active
Receiving	Giving

Tao Te Ching

The Tao Te Ching, the ancient Chinese text on the philosophy of Taoism, tells us that when people see things as beautiful, ugliness is created. When people see things as good, evil is created. Being and non-being produce each other. Difficult and easy complement each other. Long and short define each other. High and low depend upon each other. Fore and aft follow each other.

This classic teaching tells us that *this* is also *that*, and *that* is also *this*, and *this* gives birth to *that*. As long as we are qualifying or quantifying *this* or *that*, we are unable to experience the totality of existence. Thinking that *this* is better than *that* is the primary cause of suffering in our life.

Acceptance of *What Is*

Duality is painful to us primarily because we are trained to resist its authentic, organic presence in our lives. Our resistance brings on drama and conflict. Acceptance of duality means trusting that everything exists in perfection, even while it appears unpleasant and wrong. Life is not about eliminating contrast; it is about finding harmony within the spectrum.

With acceptance of *what is*, we surrender our mind's striving to control our life. As the mind calms, it is no longer screaming, denying, blaming, or judging how wrong things are or how they should be different.

Acceptance of *what is* does not mean we condone war, murder, racism or environmental destruction. However, if our focus is lost in the anger, the frustration, the despair, our energy is restricted and drained and we're not radiating love. We cannot effectively facilitate the peace and harmony we seek by perpetuating conflict and pain.

When we bring our conscious presence into the world and take creative actions that are not infused with anger, resentment or judgment, we can affect situations with our tuning fork of peaceful presence, instead of sliding into resonance with chaos and discord.

Our natural, authentic feelings were never meant to be an experience of being mired in chronic struggle, but are accurate indications of our true experience of the moment. It is through the acceptance of *what is* that we experience the richness of life.

Emotional Duality

The polarity we feel in our emotions can be debilitating. We understand that night and day complement each other and death would not exist without life, yet how are happiness and sadness dependent on each other? These emotions are actually the same vibration, residing at opposite ends of the spectrum. Emotions, like all aspects of duality, are interdependent, continually dancing in various stages of equilibrium between the swings of the pendulum. One emotion might feel better than the other, yet both are necessary for us to fully dance the ebb and flow of life.

Our family and community programmed our emotional conditioning into us at a very early age. Many of us were raised in unhealthy emotional environments, and were infused with our parents' anger, fear, and lack of self-love. We took on their unhealthy emotional behaviors and patterns and made them our own.

Many of us were taught when we were small that it was not okay to feel bad, that good girls smile pretty and that brave boys don't cry; that we should always be positive, strong, attractive, pleasant, successful, and happy. We felt wrong, damaged, or weak when we experienced what we had been taught to think of as negative emotions. Suppressing our emotions further, we learned that it was better to keep our mouths shut. Some of us, on the other hand, were rarely exposed to 'positive' expressions of emotion, and grew up believing that an environment of anger, resentment, or depression is normal. These folks had no safety or permission to fully experience their true feelings either.

E-motion is *energy in motion*. When our feelings are in motion, they simply flow through us. Emotions are meant to be expressed, not suppressed.

Candace Pert, researcher and author of *Molecules of Emotion*, has proven that neuropeptides, the chemicals triggered by emotions, physically interact with cells and tissues in our bodies. When emotions authentically move, the network pathways in the body harmonize with each other, whereas suppressed or stagnant emotions are toxic and inhibit our life force, causing dissonance or disease in the body.

The Duality of Emotions

Trust	Fear
Joy	Sadness
Acceptance	Resistance
Peace	Turmoil
Contentment	Anxiety
Gratitude	Resentment
Inspiration	Grief
Attraction	Repulsion
Delight	Anger
Exhilaration	Hopelessness
Boredom	Fascination

Experiencing Emotions Coherently

We are coherent (in alignment) with our emotions when we allow and fully experience them, without pushing them away or suppressing them. Emotional coherency is allowing the full spectrum of emotions to move through us.

Emotions are incoherent when we feel one way but show something different, often because we are trying not to feel our true feelings or we do not believe they are appropriate or safe to reveal.

In my acupuncture practice, I can tell when a client is suffering from a physical imbalance as a result of stuck emotions. They might tell me a sad story and then laugh. Or they feel frustrated and angry but insist that everything is fine. When they effectively move the stagnant emotions, their vitality increases, as their life force (love) is freed up.

When we make time to genuinely feel our emotions, we have coherency of body, mind, and spirit, which is healthy for us. When we stifle, ignore, or hide our feelings, there is confusion and incoherency in our body, causing dis-ease.

It can be healthy to have a complete emotional

breakdown or an angry explosion. Sometimes this is VERY appropriate. Welcome the emotion and allow its flow. Experience the beauty of the movement in you. Feel it totally. Cry, moan, weep, yell, throw a fit.

The mind wants to go into story (Why did this happen?... If only he hadn't...I'll never...I could only be happy if...). Story leads us to suffering.

We experience our emotions coherently by simply welcoming, embracing, and feeling the sensations in the body. Suppressed emotion is stuck love. The less we block our emotions, the more we feel our natural state: freely flowing life force and love.

Summary

- ♡ Duality is the amphitheater for physical life.

- ♡ The Yin and Yang symbol represents the union of opposites.

- ♡ Harmony comes from the acceptance of *what is*.

- ♡ Emotions are energy in motion.

♡ Suppressed and stagnant emotions cause disharmony in our bodies.

Part Two

The Elements

Don't say this is good and that is bad. Drop all discrimination. Accept everything as it is. Liberation cannot be desired because desire is the bondage. When you are desireless, you are liberated. Tantra accepts everything, lives everything. ~ Osho

Chapter Four

Ho'oponopono

Nothing is good. Nothing is bad. When this dawns in your consciousness, suddenly you are together, all fragments have disappeared into one unity... ~ Osho

*H*o'oponopono is an ancient Hawaiian and Polynesian healing art of reconciliation and forgiveness that's been used for centuries to support, correct, restore, and maintain harmonious relationships between people, Nature and Spirit. A fundamental belief is that harmony in one's external relationships begins by establishing harmony between one's own body, mind and spirit. Specific Ho'oponopono practices have developed over time and they continue to evolve to this day.

Ho'o means to cause something to happen. *Pono* means balance, goodness, righteousness, order, alignment, or harmony. Ho'oponopono translates: 'to bring into balance,' 'to bring harmony.' By repeating 'pono,' the power of the word is accentuated.

Hawaiians believe that to determine whether a thought, word, or action is 'pono,' one must consider how it affects not only our present generation of family and community, but also how it affects both our ancestors and our descendants. All life forms are inter-connected; family includes not only our human relatives and friends, but also nature. To be 'pono' on all levels, a thought, word or deed must be harmonious or beneficial to the family and the environment.

Traditional Ho'oponopono

Ho'oponopono is used traditionally by families and friends to rectify any differences, perceived wrongdoings, or conflicts amongst them. Additionally, when a person is ill or injured, the first step in the healing process is to hold a ceremonial Ho'oponopono session. The custom always begins with prayer and is led by respected family elders. Each family member is invited to share their thoughts and feelings, and all actions related to the issue at hand are brought to the light. When emotions run strong, comments are directed to the leader, rather than directly to other individuals involved in the dispute. The elder facilitates the process with questions when needed, and makes sure everyone has a chance to be heard. One or more periods of silence are taken for reflection on the entanglement of emotions and grievances. The group collectively decides and implements whatever corrective action is needed in order to restore harmony for everyone. All participants release each other and the past, and together they close the event with a ceremonial feast. Most problems and grievances have multiple dimensions and layers associated with them. Unraveling all the layers is referred to as 'peeling the onion.' Depending on the number of people involved and the layers of discord, the healing may occur in one day or it can take months before harmony is restored. These gatherings can be done daily, weekly, or as needed.

In one family tradition, for example, a 'bowl of light' is made from a gourd harvested from the garden. The top of the gourd is cut off, becoming the lid for the bowl. This beautiful gourd is placed in a special place in the home where all can see it. If someone in the family does something that is not 'pono' or in harmony with the family's shared values and protocol, the lid is put on the bowl. This is an indication that Ho'oponopono is needed. The family then comes together in truth and with an open heart, and a traditional Ho'oponopono session is held.

Self-Identity Through Ho'oponopono

In 1976 Morrnah Simeona, regarded as a Hawaiian healing priest, adapted the traditional Ho'oponopono family reconciliation practice to the social realities of the modern day.

She adapted the healing art both into a general problem solving process outside the family and into an individual (rather than group) self-inquiry and accountability process. Morrnah's version was influenced by her Christian education and her philosophical studies ranging from Chinese and Indian mysticism to the work of psychic Edgar Cayce. She considered problems to be the effects of negative karma (cause and effect), saying, "you have to experience for yourself what you have done to others," thus her process was a personal self-healing practice.

Morrnah taught, "you are the creator of your life circumstances." She called this individual form of the art *Self-Identity Through Ho'oponopono.* She explained, "We are the sum total of our experiences, which is to say that we are burdened by our pasts. When we experience stress or fear in our lives, if we would look carefully, we would find that the cause is actually a memory."

The subconscious mind associates a stimulus in the present with something that happened in the past. When this occurs, emotions are activated and stress can be produced. Morrnah continued, "The main purpose of this process is to discover the Divinity within oneself. The Ho'oponopono is a profound gift that allows one to develop a working relationship with the Divinity within and learn to ask that in each moment, our errors in thought, word, deed or action be cleansed. The process is essentially about freedom, complete freedom from the past."

This type of Ho'oponopono is based on the principle of taking total responsibility for our internal experience of life. Total responsibility means viewing everything around us as a projection from inside ourself. To change our external reality, we must first change our inner reality. Viewing all consciousness as interconnected, the premise is that when something is changed within an individual, this change is also reflected in the whole of humanity.

The function of Morrnah's practice of *Self-Identity Through Ho'oponopono* was primarily to release unhappy, negative memories and conditioning from our subconscious mind. She taught that to do this we must connect with the Divinity on a moment-to-moment basis and ask for the cleansing of all distress which that moment contains, allowing us to reclaim our personal connection with Love, our Divine Source.

Since Morrnah's passing in 1992, her former student and administrator Dr. Hew Len has continued to further her teachings.

SOME BASIC PRINCIPLES I GAINED FROM SELF-IDENTITY THROUGH HO'OPONOPONO:

- ♡ We are each responsible for our own peace and harmony.

- ♡ Disharmony is caused by memories, thought forms, DNA, and genetic programming stored in the subconscious mind.

- ♡ The physical tension that is created by the triggering of memories relaxes when I feel the vibration of love in my body.

- ♡ Everyone and everything in our life is simply a mirror of something inside ourselves.

- ♡ We can resolve any disharmony occurring in

our life by healing the stored memory that is being triggered.

♡ When I heal myself, I heal all of humanity.

Harmonizing

The type of Ho'oponopono I am offering is called *Harmonizing*. Derived from Ho'oponopono and based on the Universal Principles and Elements outlined in this book, it is a personal healing process for bringing harmony and sovereignty to one's life. The focus of this process is our relationship with our self, no one and nothing else. We *bring harmony* to the aspect of our consciousness that causes us pain and suffering.

Summary

♡ Ho'oponopono means to *bring harmony*.

♡ Ho'oponopono restores *aloha* (love) to groups or individuals.

♡ The purpose of *Harmonizing*, the form of Ho'oponopono offered in this book, is to restore our natural state of inner peace by bringing harmony and balance to our mental and emotional turmoil and our painful memories.

Chapter Five

Consciousness

The first thing to becoming a master of oneself is to become more conscious of your acts and your thoughts. Unconsciousness is slavery, consciousness is mastery... Consciousness means living with a witness; unconsciousness means living without a witness. ~ *Osho*

*C*onsciousness is how we are aware that we are alive. Our consciousness creates our experience. We perceive the world according to our focus of attention, which directs the movement of our life energy. Consciousness gives our love the opportunity to express itself.

Aspects of Mind

The mind is what controls our consciousness. Let us look at the characteristics and inter-relationships between what we are calling the 'subconscious,' 'conscious' and 'superconscious' mind.

The Subconscious Mind is the automatic aspect of our mind. It is like the hard drive or memory bank of a computer, storing all memories, learning, habitual patternings, and genetic DNA. Ninety-five percent of our thoughts are generated unconsciously from here. The subconscious is sometimes equated with the Yin principle, the more receptive or passive aspect of the self. It is at times described as the *right brain* or as the *feeling mind.*

The imprint of this aspect of our mind begins in the embryotic stage of life at the moment that the egg and sperm unite. Our genetic programming, our DNA, is passed to us in the womb, along with the imprint of our mother's thoughts, sensations, and feelings. Our subconscious contains the beliefs, codes of behavior, and assumptions about reality, which are based upon our observations and interactions with others as well as the collective patterning of previous generations.

From birth until the age of six our brains are in a theta frequency, which is very receptive. During this time we are easily influenced by everything in our environment, and what surrounds us is literally programmed into our body and mind in this first stage of life.

This programming comes from our family, neighbors, teachers, classmates, friends, church, TV, music, and the larger environment. Emotional pain that we didn't have the opportunity or safety to express and release is stored here as well.

Programmed
Stores Memories
Habitual
Yin ~ Feminine
Feeling Mind
Right Brain

Subconscious

The Conscious Mind can be likened to a processor of a computer. It is labeled as the *rational* or *reasoning* mind, where we can exercise choice in the present moment. Only 5% of our thoughts are conscious, or readily available to our awareness. The conscious mind is sometimes equated with the Yang principle, the analytical, active, or *thinking mind*, or *left brain*. It vibrates at a higher frequency than the subconscious.

Reasoning
Problem Solving
Decision Making
Yang ~ Masculine
Analytic Mind
Left Brain

Conscious

The Superconscious Mind is the home of *infinite intelligence*—the home of our all-knowing, fully empowered self, the home of complete awareness, the place of our sovereignty. It vibrates at the highest frequency of all levels of mind. This can be thought of as our universal consciousness, the part of us that is always connected to everything else, to the Divine.

Awakened
Enlightened
Sovereign
Infinite Intelligence
Seat of Our Soul

Superconscious

Holographic Conditioning

Holographic means that each part contains the whole. I use this term to describe the aspect of our subconscious mind which stores our memories as vibrational patterns like a movie of our life. Each memory is stored with its own unique vibrational signature, depending upon how we emotionally experienced the event. This emotional vibration is like a tuning fork. We hold a different tuning fork carrying each vibration, such as grief, joy, abandonment or anger. Each time we experience one of these emotions, the frequency of that tuning fork gets stronger and more powerful within us.

Each new experience is stored together with all similar memories. Many of us have had the experience of being involved in a particular activity and we have flashbacks of when we did the same or a similar activity before.

For example, you are enjoying Christmas dinner with your family, and the smells or sounds trigger a flood of memories of previous Christmases. Or, you are walking down a path that reminds you of another walk you have taken at some point in your distant past, and memories and images of your life at that time enter your thoughts. This is your holographic conditioning at play.

Tens of thousands of thoughts per day are processed by the holographic conditioning, with 95% of them happening unbeknownst to us. These thoughts are strictly habitual in how they react to the current moment. They simply replay whatever has been conditioned earlier. They reactivate the same habitual behavioral responses to life's stimuli over and over again, without any conscious thought.

Here are some examples of how our holographic conditioning can easily get triggered, and can lead us down a non-productive path.

Feeling joyful, you go for a walk in your neighborhood and suddenly get a whiff of apple pie coming from the kitchen window of a neighboring house. Instantly, it is as if you are back in your grandmother's kitchen waiting for the pie to come out of the oven. You begin thinking about your deceased grandmother and how much she loved and nurtured you. You miss her, and now that she is gone you feel sad and lonely. This loneliness triggers the recent memory of your cousin's death as well, and you start thinking about how you are getting old and may not have a lot of life left in you. These thoughts leave you feeling depressed and thinking further about all the things that are missing in your life.

Another hypothetical example might be that when you are enjoying a lovely evening with your romantic partner, feeling grateful and content with your life together, an old song comes on the radio. A song that you called 'our song' in a past relationship long ago. Passionate romantic memories are triggered, and you begin to wonder what life would have been like if you had never broken up. Looking over at your current partner, you begin to judge him and make comparisons in your mind. You begin to feel disgruntled and start a quarrel over something insignificant.

The act of worrying is one of the greatest triggers of the holographic memory bank. When we worry, frightening memories and images from the past are stirred up and projected into the future.

An example might be that you are scheduled to give a talk at work in front of your colleagues regarding a project you are presenting for approval. You're not feeling fully prepared and you are afraid they are going to ask questions you cannot answer. This has happened to you before. You are embarrassed, and you do not want to let your company down this time. You are thinking, "If that happens again I might lose my job, and the mortgage is due. It is not fair really; they do not pay me enough or give me the staff I need to function at my best. Why should I stress myself out for this corporation that doesn't even appreciate me?" This thinking makes you feel agitated and resentful, and as you feel the pain in your stomach, you're sure it is an ulcer, and you do not have medical insurance. Your thoughts continue to ramble all over the place as they continue to trigger fears... soon you're confused and lethargic.

Our current experience is constantly influenced by memories stored in our holographic conditioning.

Conscious Presence

When we break down the word *presence*, we have *pre-essence*. With 'pre' meaning 'presenting,' *presence* translates as 'the presentation of essence.' Since Love is our true essence, presence means 'presenting my love.'

Our aware presence is our most precious commodity as humans and may be the most valuable tool we have for living in sovereignty. How conscious, fully present, and aware we are in each moment is one of the only things we can actually control in life.

Most of us have little experience with being totally present in the moment. Our thinking and attention is either reflecting on the past or projecting into the future, mentally regurgitating a conversation we recently had, or anticipating an event that might occur in the future. Most of our mental chatter and worrying takes our attention away from where it could be, fully present and engaged with *what is*, in the here and now.

When we think about the past or future, we are usually drawing upon vibrational patterns from our holographic conditioning. We tend to use past conclusions and projected opinions to define the now. These mental activities actually waste our energy, when we could instead be enjoying the present moment. Choosing to live in conscious presence is a moment-by-moment endeavor.

We could say that the present moment is all there is, and all we have. Technically there is no past or future, as these concepts exist only in the mind. The past and future are projections of the mind, and this process of projecting blocks us from fully seeing and experiencing the complete range of possibilities in the present moment. The present moment is where our power resides. In the state of being in conscious awareness, we feel the free flowing life force within us, as we aren't gripped by the more stagnant, dense, and dissonant energy of the holographic conditioning, which can cause lethargy in the body. Conscious presence is a life giving, energizing experience, where we are open to possibility, creativity, and synchronicity (the beautiful and mysterious flow of life).

Collective Consciousness

Collective consciousness contains the conditioned, holographic programming of the universe, of humanity, and of all life. We live in this matrix of programming, which is constantly moving through us via neutrinos.

Neutrinos are teeny, tiny, nearly massless sub-atomic particles that travel throughout the universe carrying information. Neutrinos travel close to the speed of light and are continuously moving through us and back out into the universe. These neutrinos contain vibrational frequencies and programming that are not uniquely our own, but belong to collective consciousness. In every moment there is a constant flow of neutrinos bathing us and picking up our current emotional patterns and frequency.

This collective programming can have a strong effect on us—not unlike the unconscious effect of our own holographic conditioning.

Since we are continually influenced by the programmed matrix of the neutrino field, it behooves us to be aware that a lot of what we may be thinking and feeling is not our own. This is even more reason to practice conscious presence by choosing our focus of attention. This is exercising sovereignty.

Harmonizing Mind

In the beginning there was only one mind. In order to realize its wholeness, it had to experience separation, and so it split into two minds: the conscious (which holds our present moment awareness) and the subconscious (which holds our memories and automatic, habitual, repetitive patterns).

Our conscious, rational mind is useful for observing and recognizing the automatic, habitual patterns present in our holographic conditioning.

The conscious presence (love) can embrace the subconscious holographic conditioning (our memories of suffering). This means that we can watch our stories without believing them, identifying with them, or deciding to call them good or bad.

Witnessing (without believing) the stories of our lives is an act of consciously watching our consciousness. In the center of this embrace calmly sits our superconscious mind, the portal to our sovereignty, our awakened, enlightened nature.

In the Harmonizing practice outlined in this book, we utilize the vibration of our conscious presence to embrace and harmonize with our holographic conditioning. It's when these two aspects of our consciousness unite and come into sympathetic resonance with each other that we experience our superconscious mind. In other words, as we shine our presence of love upon the suffering of our holographic conditioning (subconscious mind), it quiets and harmonizes with our presence (conscious mind), and we have entered the portal to our Sovereignty (superconscious mind.)

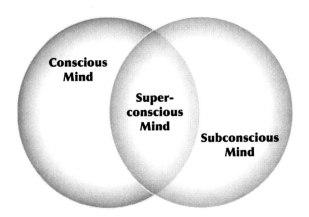

Summary

♡ Consciousness is awareness.

♡ The subconscious mind is automatic and conditioned.

♡ The conscious mind is rational and present.

♡ The superconscious is the home of infinite intelligence.

♡ Holographic conditioning stores memories as vibrational patterns.

♡ Presence ~ the presentation of essence, of love

♡ When our conscious presence embraces our holographic conditioning, we come home to the superconscious mind.

Chapter Six

Self-Responsibility

*A man of consciousness responds, and his responses
are spontaneous. He is mirrorlike: he reflects whatso-
ever confronts him. And out of this spontaneity, out
of this consciousness, a new kind of action is born.
That action never creates any bondage, any karma.
That action frees you. You remain in freedom if you
listen to your nature... ~ Osho*

Self-responsibility is claiming our ability to live life fully. It is a swift pathway to embodying our sovereignty.

Self-responsibility is the practice of acknowledging our role as the caretaker of our emotional, mental, physical, and spiritual well being; knowing that we are the creators of our life, in every moment. Self-responsibility is the opposite of blaming someone else for what we feel or experience. No one has any control over us, because we do not assign them the responsibility for making us happy. Likewise, we don't take responsibility for anyone else's happiness either. In allowing others their experience, we respect their sovereignty, the power of their own right to choose self-responsibility.

Ability to Respond

Responsibility is literally the *ability to respond*. When the autopilot of our holographic conditioning is in control, we *react* through the veil of our habitual patterns. We can *react* by force of habit or we can *respond* with our conscious presence.

A *Choice Moment* is that split second when we realize that we have a choice in how we will view, interpret, and relate to the present situation.

Have you ever believed or insisted that someone else caused your emotional state? "I am angry because once again my mother told me I would never amount to anything." Or, "I am really upset because I had planned all week to go to dinner with my partner and now tonight he has backed out." Or, "The neighbor's barking dog kept me awake all last night." The truth is that in all of these scenarios, you are upset or angry because you hold a judgment about *What Is, What Should Be,* or *How Others Should Act.* You are blaming someone else for your frustration or pain. In actuality, nothing on the outside is ever responsible for our emotional state on the inside. We are the one who holds the key to our own well being, at all times.

By observing our emotional states and our upset reactions, we can see our holographic conditioning at work. Anytime we are suffering we can ask ourselves: *What am*

I resisting? Why am I resisting it? What story am I telling myself about it? What does it remind me of? When have I felt this way before? How can I take responsibility for it right now?

Self-Responsibility Is Letting Go of Blame

In our everyday conversations we hear a lot of judgment and blame. "I was late because there was traffic." "I am miserable because it has been raining for 3 days." "I do not have any money because I had to pay my taxes." "I can't go tonight because my partner doesn't want to." "I have a headache because my child was a brat all day." When we start to pay attention to our speech, we notice how much we give others power over our inner experience. True freedom and power come from taking responsibility for each temptation to blame someone or something for how we feel.

The truth is, the less we judge others, the less we judge ourselves. Conversely, the less we judge ourselves, the less we judge others. When we get upset, it is usually because a painful thought or memory has been triggered by the current situation, and we are labeling what is happening as *bad or wrong*.

The very act of judgment means that we are not accepting *What Is*. By recognizing when we are thinking, "This should be different than it is," we arrive at a *Choice Moment*: an opportunity to choose not to go down our habitual groove of reaction, but to embrace the moment with our presence.

Harmony comes when we offer our love, attention, and presence to ourselves while we feel the irritation that has been triggered until it naturally subsides.

Acceptance of *What Is, What Was,* and *What Might Be*

Acceptance of what *is, what was, and what might be* miraculously transmutes suffering into harmony. Our level of peace is in direct proportion to our level of acceptance.

Acceptance means bringing our light of aware presence to the situation. Just this in itself can help transform any dissonance we're feeling.

Acceptance of *What Is*

Acceptance doesn't necessarily mean that we're in agreement; often we're not. We simply acknowledge that something is happening. We're OK with it because it's what is. We make this choice because relaxation feels better in our body than resistance.

Acceptance of *What Was*

Acceptance of the past brings harmony in the present.

As long as we carry pain or resentment, we hold a dissonant tuning fork that will constantly get triggered. We continue to carry that dissonant frequency until we offer our loving presence to the memory of our original pain. We also understand that the actions of others were simply reactions to their own dissonant tuning forks. Once we accept what happened, we have freed up more life force, more love, and we're more available to receive the richness of the moment.

Acceptance of *What Might Be*

Instead of worrying about what might happen in the future to cause us more suffering, we trust the Mystery of Life. We enjoy the freedom of embracing life as it unfolds, instead of trying to control the outcome.

When we relax and allow what is, we welcome and actually look forward to whatever comes, because we know we can choose to see its gift. We trust that everyone and everything that presents itself in our life has appeared for our benefit—an opportunity for us to give and receive more love.

Summary

♡ Responsibility is the *ability to respond* instead of react.

♡ Self-responsibility heals and empowers us.

♡ Self-responsibility means that no person or circumstance has any control over us.

♡ Acceptance of *what is* brings harmony and freedom.

Exercises

CHOICE MOMENT REFLECTION

Think of something you have an emotional charge about.

Ask yourself:

What am I not accepting, or telling myself should be different than it is?

Do I have an expectation, judgment or assumption about how it should be?

Am I in my holographic conditioning or in my conscious presence?

What do I consciously choose to do now?

"I" REFLECTION

Utilize this exercise when you find yourself in a reactive pattern of judgment or blame towards another. If you are judging and using the word "they," "he," or "she," you are not taking responsibility for your experience. Examples: "he should have done this," or, "she was disrespectful and unfair," or, "they are irresponsible with money," or, "she was unkind and selfish." Experiment with replacing the word "they," "he" or "she" with the word "I." An example might be the sentence: "He is being unkind and selfish," changed to: "I have been unkind and selfish." Example 2: "He does not love me," changed to, "I do not love myself." Example 3: "They've not been responsible with money," changed to, "I haven't been responsible with money."

Chapter Seven

Holographic Universe

We are all the mirror as well as the face in it. ~ *Rumi*

*Q*uantum Physics reveals that matter does not exist; that the substance of the universe is actually con-sciousness, and the act of witnessing or observing the world is what creates it. This is the interplay between consciousness and matter.

Holographic theory helps us to conceptualize life as a holographic projection that is constantly orchestrating itself to resonate with our inner reality.

Basic Hologram

A basic hologram is a three-dimensional photographic image created by energy interference patterns and laser beams.

To make a hologram, the object to be photographed is first immersed in the light of a coherent (intelligible, clear, focused) laser beam. This beam is split. One part is deflected toward the film plate and the second beam is bounced off the object and reflected onto a mirror. When

Components of a Hologram

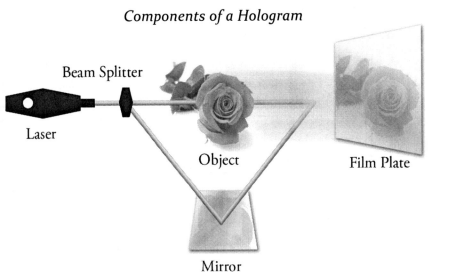

Laser · Beam Splitter · Object · Mirror · Film Plate

the beams reconverge, they form a light interference pattern which is captured on film. This is the holographic image.

If the hologram created is cut in half and then illuminated by a laser, each half will still be found to contain the entire image. If the halves are divided again, each piece of film will always be found to contain a smaller but intact version of the original image.

As an example: if an image of a rose is cut into small pieces, each piece of the holographic rose shows a three-dimensional image of the entire rose. When you shine a laser light on any piece of the rose, the entire rose is visible.

Here is another example: A cell of the human body is holographic in nature, as each cell has the complete DNA sequence required to produce the entire body.

A simple description of a hologram is this: a pattern that is whole and complete in itself and at the same time is part of an even greater pattern. Each element of the greater hologram mirrors all other elements of the pattern. Every piece contains the essence of the whole.

Holographic Consciousness

Our holographic consciousness is like the rose fragment of the hologram; every part contains the whole. For example, each specific emotional state contains all of the memories associated with that particular emotion, which means that you cannot feel one separate instant of an emotion without all your related experiences of that emotion being activated inside of you. This is the domino effect: push one domino, and each domino in the entire row falls in sequence.

Just as when we shine a laser on a fragment of the rose hologram and the entire rose is illuminated, when we focus our attention (our laser) onto an emotion or experience, all similar memories stored in our holographic consciousness are also illuminated. It is like triggering a symphony of tuning forks that resonate on the same note as the *feeling fork* of the current moment.

As the past *feeling forks* get activated, our current experience becomes amplified, creating more internal charge and intensity of feelings which are not actually relevant to the current circumstance. An example might be when we quarrel with our partner, and feel unheard, sad or frustrated. This will trigger the memories of all similar experiences that we have had in previous relationships with partners, friends, or family members, even if we are not conscious of this occurring within us. The consequence is that all of a sudden, one quarrel is magnified by another dozen previous experiences of a similar frequency, which then takes us into a downward emotional spiral.

Another example might be: when you are having a disagreement with your boss and she is starting to express her anger, it triggers a memory of your father getting very angry. Another tuning fork goes off from when your sister was angry when you were young, and before long there are numerous tuning forks building in volume in your subconscious mind. The emotional resonance becomes so strong that you are no longer able to stay consciously present in the current moment with what is really happening, which by itself is fairly minor.

Our holographic consciousness has thousands of smaller holograms within it that record and store all comparable experiences together. For example, every time we eat apple pie, ride a bike, go hiking, swimming, skiing, or attend birthday parties or family reunions, the new data resonates in harmony with the previous times we have engaged in that same activity; the apple pie or hiking hologram.

There Is No *Out There*. There is *Only You*.

All of our life experiences are a reflection of what is going on within us. We can recognize something in the world or in another person only because it exists within us as well. There is no such thing as *out there*.

Holographic theory asserts that everything we perceive is simply a mirror of our internal environment and that we create the hologram of our life by mirroring our inner state of consciousness onto the world. Our outer world is therefore a direct reflection of our inner. If our inner world is one of turmoil, then we can expect our outer world to be tumultuous as well; and inner peace generates outer peace.

Let us use the model of a hologram to look at how our Consciousness creates our reality.

The laser projects its coherent light onto the object in front of us (*what is*). The splitter then splits the light. One beam goes right through the object. The second beam of light (our focus of attention), is directed into a mirror (our state of consciousness). The image (filtered through our state of consciousness) is then reflected onto the film plate (reality as we see it). This is how we perceive what is in front of us.

When our focus is in resonance with our coherent conscious presence, the mirror will reflect exactly *what is* in front of us, a beautiful rose. However, when we are in resonance with the conditioned, habitual aspects of our holographic conditioning while perceiving the object, the image in the mirror will get distorted due to the projection of our previously stored memories, opinions, feelings, judgments, pain, and so on. We see an ugly wilted rose.

Hologram of Conscious Presence

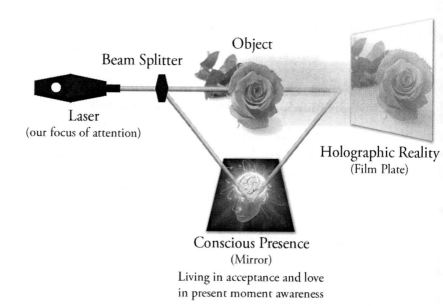

Object

Beam Splitter

Laser
(our focus of attention)

Holographic Reality
(Film Plate)

Conscious Presence
(Mirror)
Living in acceptance and love
in present moment awareness

Hologram of Holographic Conditioning

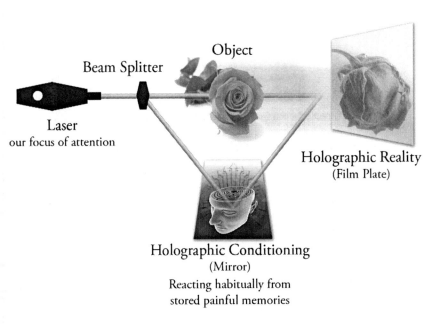

Object

Beam Splitter

Laser
our focus of attention

Holographic Reality
(Film Plate)

Holographic Conditioning
(Mirror)
Reacting habitually from
stored painful memories

In summary, our focus of awareness is projected onto a mirror (holographic conditioning or conscious presence), which creates our holographic reality.

Taking the diagrams at the right to another level, we see how our reality affects our body's crystalline structure.

Collective Hologram

Physicist David Bohm's work indicates that the universe is holographic in nature. The hologram concept is that every piece is an exact representation of the whole and can be used to reconstruct the entire hologram. The universe thus appears as a web of inseparable energy patterns containing the collective consciousness, which is a part of us, and we a part of it.

This holographic energy field has been referred to as the *Divine Matrix* (Gregg Braden), *Unified Field* (Nassim Haramein), *Unified Theory* (Albert Einstein), *The Force* (Star Wars), *Quantum Field* (Bruce Lipton), *Field of Infinite Possibility* (Deepak Chopra), *The Field* (Lynne McTaggert), and *Source Field* (David Wilcock.)

We are all intricately connected and woven together as individually unique and irreplaceable fibers in the

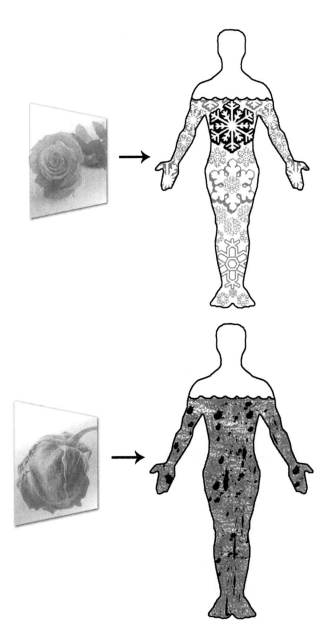

collective web of humanity. Just as each cell of our body contains a complete and detailed image of our entire self, we too are individuated cells in the body of creation, containing within us the blueprint of the Universe.

As we harmonize and bring our individual holograms into their highest vibration, this is reflected into the collective hologram. If we make one tiny change in our personal consciousness, this is repeated throughout the rest of the web. This is the beauty and possibility of the holographic model of consciousness. Change initiated anywhere in the system is mirrored throughout the entire system.

Hundredth-Monkey Phenomenon

There is a story that illustrates how each of us affects the whole.

A tribe of monkeys in Japan were given sweet potatoes dipped in sand. Disliking the sand, one monkey discovered that he could dip the potato in water and wash off the sand. After observing this for several years, other monkeys began doing the same. Suddenly they ALL began to wash off their potatoes, and after some time monkeys on other remote islands began washing their potatoes too. That is why such a spontaneous collective turn in behavior is called 'the 100th monkey,' which is also referred to as a 'tipping point.'

Another example is what is referred to as a 'flashover,' which happens when a fire burns so hot that everything in the room reaches incredibly high temperatures, and at a critical point everything simultaneously ignites.

Collective Sympathetic Resonance

There is a story about an expedition to South America led by explorer Ferdinand Magellan in the 1500's. Apparently this accounting of his travels was found in his own personal diary. Having discovered a small island, some of the crew left their large ships at sea and sailed ashore in smaller boats. The indigenous people greeted them on shore. When asked where they came from, the explorers pointed out to sea at their ships. Having never seen ships of this size, the natives reportedly could literally not see the large ships at all. They could, however, see the small boats that Magellan's crew used to row up to shore, as they were similar to the natives' own canoes.

The tribe's shaman was fascinated by the possibility of seeing something for which he had no previous framework or reference point. After great effort, he was finally able to see the ships. A few days later, others on the island began to benefit from the shift in their shaman's perception. As consciousness worked and spread holographically, they too gained the ability to see the ships.

Collective Sympathetic Resonance means that when one person makes a change in their consciousness, it creates a new pattern in the collective consciousness, which supports others to experience the same shift within. Another way of looking at this is that the natives' individual tuning forks of consciousness came into sympathetic resonance with the tuning fork of their shaman.

There are various philosophies around the world which speak of the possibility or probability of a time when humanity will experience world peace, when collectively humans will live primarily in conscious presence. As we individually change our holograms from a reality of conflict to one of harmony, a critical mass may eventually cause a tipping point, bringing us all into *collective sympathetic resonance* with a reality of peace and harmony. This is my prayer for humanity.

Summary

- ♡ Life is holographic: each part contains the whole.

- ♡ Our memories are stored as a hologram.

- ♡ Our outer world is a mirror of our internal state.

- ♡ As any part changes, the whole changes.

Chapter Eight

Heart

Heart is the transcendence of duality... it sees things clearly, and love is its natural quality... the heart knows nothing of the past, nothing of the future; it knows only of the present... ~ Osho

The Emperor

*T*he heart is the first organ formed in the fetus. It beats its first beat before the physical brain is formed. With its own receptors, nervous system, nerve ganglia and electromagnetic force, the heart is 45-70 times more powerful than the physical brain.

The Chinese consider the heart to be the Supreme Controller, the Emperor of our physical kingdom. The 'Nei Ching,' the Internal Medicine Classic, states: "The heart commands all of the organs and viscera, houses the spirit, and controls the emotions." The Chinese word for heart is also used to denote mind.

Our heart is the home of our soul and the seat of our deepest intelligence. The heart's vibrational frequency is that of love. It's like a tuning fork in sympathetic resonance with our essence. When we unite our presence (our full attention and awareness) with our heart, we are able to consciously experience the physical embodiment of our essence.

The heart receives information via its intuitive, feeling nature, as well as through complex physical systems of communication, not through a mental thinking process. Through this feeling and body chemistry network, the information processed in the heart is then transmitted to the physical brain.

The electromagnetism of the heart is strongly influenced by our instinctual and intuitive awareness, and it is through our feelings that this electromagnet entrains the rest of our body. When our feelings and emotions are in harmony, so is the heart's electromagnetic field, which spreads out 15-16' beyond the boundaries of the physical body. The heart's intelligence is clearly demonstrated in heart transplant patients, as they often end up with memories and personality traits of their donors, due to the cellular memory stored in the heart cells. For example, a transplant recipient, who has been a vegetarian all his life and regularly practices yoga, finds himself craving McDonalds hamburgers and wanting to go to boxing matches. Often the vocabulary of a heart transplant recipient changes dramatically as well.

Heart's Electromagnetic Field

Heart Coherency

The Institute of HeartMath is a research and education organization dedicated to helping people reduce stress and self-regulate their emotions. HeartMath's research has advanced the knowledge of heart-brain interactions and heart-rhythm coherence, showing us that the heart has specific beat patterns that are either coherent or incoherent, meaning harmonious or chaotic.

Our heart-rhythm patterns are linked to our emotional states and the sensations they generate in our body, as well as the electromagnetic energy field that surrounds our body. Emotions such as affection, contentment, gratitude, and delight radiate coherent patterns, whereas feelings such as dread, despair, frustration, and resentment radiate incoherent patterns, which cause dissonance or stress in the body.

A coherent heart rhythm pattern indicates a state of balance and synchronization between both parts of our autonomic nervous system, the sympathetic and parasympathetic. This harmonious pattern is called 'heart coherency,' and in this state all the cells in the body dance together in physiological harmony. Within seconds of arriving in this state of heart coherency, other electrical rhythms in the body are entrained, synchronizing our brain, nervous system, organs, and glands.

Coherency (meaning order, harmonious function, harmonious connection with all parts) of the heart happens when we are consciously present and relaxed.

Hormonal Heart

The heart releases hormones in response to our thoughts and feelings. Some of the hormones secreted are dopamine, epinephrine and oxytocin. Oxytocin is commonly referred to as the 'love and bonding hormone,' and is primarily known for its activity during childbirth, lactation, and sexual and non-sexual intimate connections. A recent study found that when a person engages in a conscious hug with another, oxytocin is released after 20 seconds.

The more we feel the flow of love and gratitude inside ourselves through fostering loving and nurturing connections with ourselves and others, the more we release this 'love hormone.' Oxytocin decreases stress, blood pressure, and cravings, and increases a sensation of relaxation and deep calm. It encourages a sensation of melting into a warm pool of peaceful, blissful surrender.

An influence of duality on our life is the polarity we often experience between our heart and mind, between our feeling nature and our thinking process. We may get a message or feeling from our heart's intelligence, but instead of trusting this feeling, we go into a thought process with our mind, which is usually influenced by our holographic conditioning. Choices made from our heart's intelligence are actually more life serving.

We can effectively harmonize our heart and mind by inviting our mental thought or agitation to relax into the expanded wisdom that is our coherent heart, the home of our soul.

Summary

♡ The vibration of the heart is in sympathetic resonance with love.

♡ The heart is the Emperor of our body and houses our soul.

♡ Heart intelligence is perceived through feeling, not thinking.

♡ Heart coherency is dependent on a healthy emotional state.

♡ Heart coherency entrains our body, creating a harmonious physical state of well-being.

Exercise

HEART COHERENCY

Relaxing and following your breath entrains your heart rhythm with your breath rhythm. This leads to heart coherency. The following is most effective when done for at least 5 minutes.

Place your hand on your heart and bring your full awareness here.

Breathe into the area of your heart, slowly and deeply.

Follow your gentle breath—5 seconds in and five seconds out. Do this several times.

Activate a feeling of love and gratitude by thinking of someone or something that helps generate this feeling in your heart.

Allow this feeling of love and gratitude to build in your heart. After a few moments you can begin to radiate this feeling out into your entire body.

Chapter Nine

Sacred Geometry

The only way out of ignorance and out of this dark night of the soul is to be aware of your own being, aware of your own awareness. In that moment when you are aware of your own awareness, everything stops, time stops. Suddenly you are beyond time and beyond space, and a door opens which makes you part of the whole... ~ Osho

One morning when I was sitting in meditation on the top of my favorite mountain on Kauai, spontaneously an image came into my mind's eye forming two circles, one on each side of my head. Merging together, they overlapped, forming an almond shape on the center of my forehead. All of my awareness gravitated to this area. My consciousness expanded beyond anything I'd ever experienced. It was like I'd gone through a portal to a blissful awareness of infinite spaciousness and timelessness. Months later I shared my experience with a friend who told me that this shape was the fundamental shape of all Sacred Geometry and was called the Vesica Piscis. This began my research into Sacred Geometry and the deepening of my experience with this portal to the infinite.

*S*acred Geometry contains certain mathematical relationships which radiate vibrational frequencies that call their surrounding environment into resonance with their high vibration of perfect harmony.

The Vesica Piscis

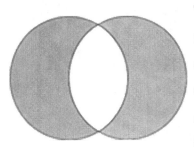

The Vesica Piscis is the most basic and important construction in Sacred Geometry. The shape is derived from the intersection of two identical circles. An ancient symbol of transformation, it represents the merging of duality, heaven and earth, masculine and feminine, yin and yang, spirit and body. It is the basic motif for the 'flower of life,' a geometric figure composed of multiple evenly-spaced overlapping circles, arranged to form a flower-like pattern.

The Flower of Life

The Latin term *Vesica Piscis* means 'The Vessel of the Fish.' The Pythagorean 'measure of the fish' is a mystical symbol representing the intersection of spirit and matter.

Referred to as the root geometry of the universe, the Vesica Piscis contains the circle, the triangle, the tetrad, the square, the pentacle, and many more polygons, which make it a true symbolic womb.

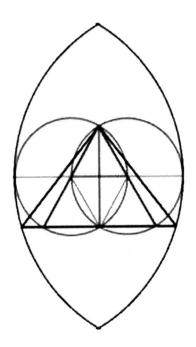

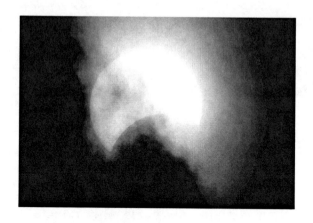

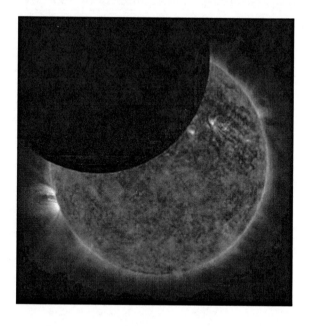

*A Solar Eclipse is a beautiful image of
the merging of Yin (moon) and Yang (sun).*

The Vesica Piscis represents divine union. Its two identical, interlocking circles signify two polarities, the magnetic and electric, coming together to form a trinity. This sacred geometric pattern occurs both when a star explodes in the heavens and in the moment when the first two cells of new life divide in the human womb.

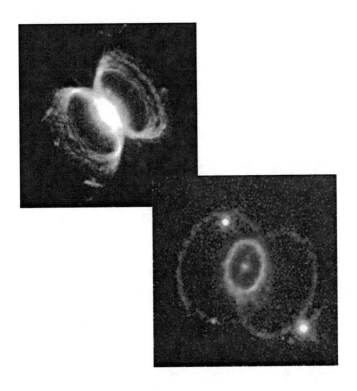

Vesica Piscis Nebulae are formed when a star explodes.

Sacred Union—Seed of Life

Life begins as a sphere. The female's ovum is a perfect circle. Within this circle is another perfect circle known as the female pronucleus. It contains only half of the chromosomes needed to create a fetus, and awaits the perfectly matching sperm containing the other half of the chromosomes.

Once the ovum accepts the sperm, the sperm begins the swim toward the female pronucleus. The tail of the sperm breaks off, and the head immediately begins to expand into a perfect sphere, which is called the male pronucleus. The sphere continues to expand until it becomes exactly the same size as the female pronucleus, and as they unite, they form a Vesica Piscis.

The male pronucleus continues permeating the female pronucleus until they become unified. This becomes the first cell of the human body, a human zygote. The cells continue to divide and form what is called an 'egg of life' that is identical to the 'Flower of Life' sacred geometric pattern.

The creation of the Flower of Life perfectly mirrors the cellular beginning of human life.

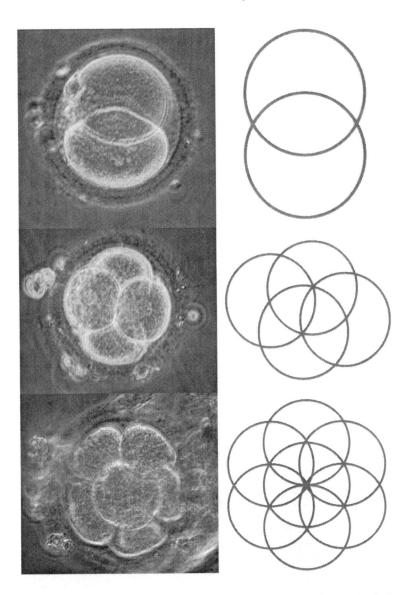

Left: Human embryo cells dividing to form an 'egg of life.'
Right: Vesica Piscis repeated to form a 'flower of life.'

Sacred Architecture

The Vesica Piscis can be found in the ornamentation on nearly every medieval church in Europe. Many of these churches were devoted to the Virgin Mary or Mary Magdalene. The Vesica Piscis decorates portal sculpture on churches celebrating the Sacred Feminine, such as the Chapel of St. Mary and the Chalice Well cover located In Glastonbury, England.

St. Mary's, Bristol, England

Chalice Well cover

Mandorla

The Mandorla (Italian for *almond*) is a Vesica Piscis shaped halo that envelopes the whole body, signifying a greater degree of sanctity and divine power than a regular halo. The Mandorla is often seen surrounding Christ in representations of the Transfiguration, Ascension and Last Judgment, as well as in depictions of the Virgin Mary.

Christ's ascension in the mandorla

Virgin Mary in the mandorla

In Pagan times, the Vesica Piscis was associated with the love Goddess Venus or Aphrodite, and represented fertility and the sacred feminine, evidenced by its resemblance to the vagina and the womb.

The Vesica Piscis provides us with an inner doorway or portal to our ultimate 'Home,' the place where duality and separateness cease to exist. Through the geometry of the Vesica Piscis, a very specific vibrational portal is created. When we surround ourselves in this geometry, we benefit from its vibrational power and amplify our personal vibration of wholeness and oneness.

Summary

The Vesica Piscis is:

- ♡ The root geometry of the universe
- ♡ A portal between heaven and earth—a doorway home
- ♡ The point that unifies duality
- ♡ A vibration that amplifies personal sense of wholeness

Exercises

VESICA PISCIS

This meditation guides you into feeling the vibration of the portal that's generated by the geometry of the Vesica Piscis.

BASIC PRACTICE

Sit comfortably in an upright position. Allow your body to relax. Take a few deep breaths. Continue to follow your breath for a few moments.

Direct your attention to the top of your head. Begin feeling energy on the crown of your head.

Visualize two spheres, one on each side of your head. These spheres are about the size of your head. Following your breath, relax more deeply.

Slowly visualize the spheres coming together at the center of your forehead, just above your eyes, at your third eye. They will begin to overlap as they gradually form a Vesica Piscis. The space where they overlap surrounds your third eye.

Begin to feel the pulse of energy in your third eye, the center of the Vesica Piscis. Bring all of your awareness into this sacred vibration... just Be in this energy.

Whatever experience you have is perfect for you. It's a little different for everyone.

VESICA PISCIS HEART COHERENCY

EXPANDING ON THE BASIC PRACTICE...

Allow the Vesica Piscis to slowly drop from your forehead down your body into your heart space, allowing your outbreath to expand the Vesica Piscis around your heart, and your inbreath to deepen your relaxation. Feel the vibration of the Vesica Piscis come into resonance with your heartbeat.

Stay here as long as you like.

MANDORLA OR FULL BODY VESICA PISCIS

The Vesica Piscis is embracing your heart. Let it grow and expand until it envelops your entire body. You may experience it as a pulsating three-dimensional almond shaped orb as it surrounds you.

Part Three

Harmonizing

Your task is not to seek for love,
but merely to seek and find all the barriers within yourself
that you have built against it. ~ Rumi

Chapter Ten

Harmonizing the Split in Consciousness

Become conscious of your consciousness. And in that very becoming, in that very silence—when you are only conscious of your consciousness and not of any other content—no thought, no desire, no dream—you are just conscious of your being conscious... you become aware of the divine, you become aware of the essential core of your being. ~ Osho

*W*e are born totally present, totally whole, fully connected to the Great Oneness of Existence. When the cord to our mother is cut, we meet the impact of Duality. Our consciousness splits. All we knew was wholeness, completeness, and suddenly there is something else: separation—aloneness.

We gradually lose contact with our pure nature as the environment, the world of contrast, programs our mind. We grow away from our inner presence and believe that the external world is all there is. This experience of separation is what forms our holographic conditioning, the stones in our bowl of light.

We feel that something is missing. We long for the unconditional love and unbroken oneness that we knew prior to emerging into the realm of duality. We reach out into the world searching for something that will fulfill this emptiness, when all the while it has been resting within us.

Harmonizing is a practice that repairs this split and satisfies our sense of separation. It is the reunion of the two aspects of our consciousness, our holographic conditioning with our conscious presence.

This is like returning to the Great Womb where everything is taken care of, all is well, all our needs are met, and we bask again in the feeling of oneness that we felt prior to separation. This homecoming is our return to the Sovereignty of Love.

The split in our consciousness could be likened to a separation between a parent and child, a relationship that's suffered from lack of communication, love, and intimacy. Without these vital ingredients, the child suffers and will eventually perish from lack of nurturing.

If a child feels alone and unseen, she may act out and demand attention, often by misbehaving. Our painful conditioning is the same; it too wants love and attention. The healing of our split in consciousness is dependent on a healthy, communicative relationship between our holographic conditioning and our conscious presence. We create this by becoming the conscious caretaker of our painful conditioning.

Let's experience this by imagining our conscious

presence as a loving, conscious parent and our holographic conditioning as an unhappy child.

When a child is upset, screaming and crying, and the parent is right there giving loving attention to the child, it will eventually calm down. When the tuning fork of presence is unwavering and strong, the dissonant fork of the child's distress will eventually come into resonance with its parent's calm and gentle tuning fork. The connection between them is so deeply satisfying that the child (our holographic conditioning) falls back into its natural state of innocence, trust, and joy.

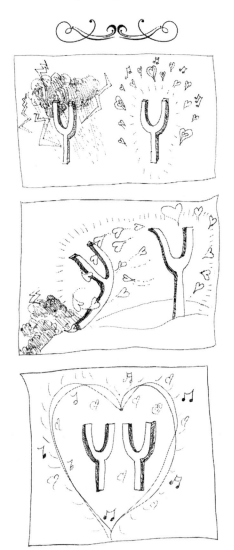

*Our Conscious Presence calling our
Holographic Conditioning into Resonance with Love.*

Our conscious relationship with our holographic conditioning requires absolute vigilance and presence. With the sweetness of our unconditional compassion for our pain and compulsion, we develop a very deep, ever-expanding love affair founded on trust, intimacy, vulnerability, surrender, acceptance and patience. This deep, loving connection with Self is the template for all other relationships, the one we have with our partner, our children and our grandchildren, nature, and ultimately, all of Existence.

This sacred embrace between our Conscious Presence (parent) and our Holographic Conditioning (child) forms a Vesica Piscis, the portal to our Sovereignty of Love, our awakened, enlightened state, our sense of connection with the love of the Universe.

This doesn't mean that we arrive somewhere absolute and static. We are not eliminating our holographic conditioning or residing permanently in our conscious presence. It's this split in consciousness that's given us the physical human experience of duality. We will always be dancing in and out of the spheres of consciousness, between contraction and expansion. It is in this dance of ebb and flow that we experience all of who we are. Living in sovereignty is the empowered state of knowing our way to the portal home, through the Vesica Piscis to our essence, in any given moment.

Chapter Eleven

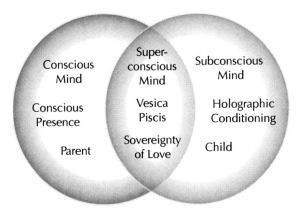

Weaving it All Together

*A man who is aware cannot move in the past, because
it is no more. A man who is aware cannot move in
the future, because it is not yet. A man who is aware
lives in the present, herenow. Here is his only space,
and now is his only time. And because he is only
herenow, time as such disappears. Eternity is born,
timelessness is born.* ~ *Osho*

*T*he primary components of the Harmonizing Practice are the Principles and Elements we have covered so far.

Let's briefly review them now.

The Principles

Love is the source and essence of all creation.

Vibration is the energy that makes up matter, thoughts, and emotions. Like attracts like.

Duality allows the human experience of contrast, the amphitheater in which life experiences itself.

The Elements

Ho'oponopono is an art of reconciliation that restores love and harmony.

Consciousness is the awareness with which we can differentiate between conditioned programming and sovereign presence in the moment.

Self-Responsibility is accepting *What Is* and claiming authorship of our lives.

Holographic Universe means that the outer world is a perfect reflection of the inner, and that a change in any part affects the whole.

Heart, the seat of our deepest intelligence, is the physical space in our body where we can most easily commune with the vibrational frequency of our essence, love.

Vesica Piscis is the unifying point of duality and the sacred geometric portal through which lies the ultimate state of wholeness, our Sovereignty of Love.

Embodying the Elements

How do we apply these concepts to our daily life?

Embodiment of The Elements		
Doesn't Look Like	**Element**	**Looks Like**
✗ Feeling controlled by others ✗ Resistance to *What Is* ✗ Blaming others for emotions ✗ Self-judgment	**Self-Responsibility**	♪ Freedom ♪ Acceptance of *What Is* ♪ Welcoming emotions ♪ Self-love
✗ Telling myself a story ✗ Reacting habitually	**Consciousness**	♪ Present moment awareness ♪ Responding consciously
✗ Body dissonance (tension) ✗ Mental agitation ✗ Loneliness	**Heart**	♪ Heart coherency (relaxation) ♪ Heart intelligence (wisdom) ♪ Feels like home
✗ Feeling conflicted ✗ Holding onto a judgment ✗ Blocked life force	**Ho'oponopono**	♪ Peace of mind ♪ Releasing painful memories ♪ Restoring the flow of love
✗ Something *out there* creates my reality ✗ I'm separate and alone	**Holographic Universe**	♪ Everything is a mirror of what's in me ♪ A change in me is a change in humanity
✗ Chaos and fragmentation ✗ Separation ✗ Fear	**Vesica Piscis**	♪ An energetic portal to Universal love ♪ Sovereignty (aware of wholeness) ♪ Held in soft, safe, warm embrace

Chapter Twelve

The Harmonizing Phrase

Transforming unconsciousness into consciousness—
that is the real transformation of base metal into gold.
Gold represents consciousness, enlightenment. ~ Osho

"I Love You, Thank You, Please Come Home to Love"

*T*his phrase is used as a communication between the two spheres of our consciousness. The conscious presence (awareness in the moment) is speaking to the holographic conditioning (our recurring pain and compulsion). It is a primary component of the Harmonizing Practice.

When someone is suffering, we want to nurture them, ultimately to bring them into sympathetic resonance with the tuning fork of love. This is the purpose of the Harmonizing Phrase—to consciously offer our love to the aspects of our holographic conditioning that are suffering, be it emotionally, mentally, or physically. We welcome the pain or conflict that's arisen, so that we can share our compassion and love with it, and invite the distressed part of ourselves to return to its original frequency, love.

We are saying:

I Love You to the painful memory that has been triggered, the injured part of myself that is needing love and causing me dissonance (emotional, mental, or physical).

Thank You to the injured, vulnerable part of myself for revealing itself and gifting me with the opportunity to heal.

Please Come Home to Love invites the dissonant, stuck energy of the memory to return back into the resonance of love.

We use the Harmonizing Phrase as a mantra (a chant repeated deliberately for the purpose of changing the state of consciousness and relaxing the body) to harmonize our split in consciousness. It takes us out of the mind and into the heart by radiating the high vibration of these words into the body.

We're talking to the vibration in our body via the

vibration of the words. Frequency communicating with frequency. The feeling of love and gratitude infuses itself into our body and harmonizes the dissonant vibrations. We release the mental thought and go directly to the feeling of the pain; taking a tuning fork that is singing an old sad song out of tune and calling it back into sweet harmony.

Sincerely feeling the energy and kindness of the words is as important as the words themselves. As the words are felt and spoken, a resonant vibration sings out into the body. This frees up stagnant and dissonant energy (stuck love) as it comes into sympathetic resonance with the frequency of love and gratitude.

As you actively use this phrase, you will find for yourself what it means to you and what you are addressing when you speak and feel it. It's different for each person, and will deepen and expand as you use it.

There are times when the subconscious mind excessively processes a thought as it habitually loops and regurgitates a story and its accompanying fears, going on and on. The chatter seems impossible to stop; yet it's just the dissonant cacophony of tuning forks going off in the subconscious. By using the Harmonizing Phrase over and over again like a mantra, we reclaim choice of our thoughts. This is a tool for fully focusing our attention and directing it to the moment at hand, superseding the subconscious babble's control over us. When we're not consciously present in the moment, the subconscious is in control.

Chapter Thirteen

Turning Stones into Crystals

Every atom, every molecule, every group of atoms and molecules, however simple or complex, however large or small, tells the story of itself, its pattern, its purpose, through the vibrations which emanate from it...
Thus at any time, in any world, a soul will give off through vibrations the story of itself and the condition in which it now exists. ~ Edgar Cayce

Harmonizing

*H*armonizing is a practice to heal the stones in our bowl of light—to transform them into crystals.

Harmonizing is a way of life. It's a moment-to-moment practice of remembering the principles (we are *love, vibrating* in a realm of *duality*) and employing the elements in order to create, cultivate, and nurture a harmonious life.

The principle of the Harmonizing Practice is to witness our emotions when they arise and bring our body's consciousness into sympathetic resonance with the vibration of love. The following processes give us the steps to actualize the practice of Harmonizing.

The Harmonizing Practice

Notice your emotional and mental state.

Observe the circumstance currently presenting itself.

Be present with yourself.

Accept what is.

Claim the situation as your own creation, a mirror from within.

Place your hand on your heart and bring your awareness to your heart.

Welcome your feelings into your heart.

Breathe slowly and deeply, breathing in love, exhaling peace.

Radiate love and peace throughout your body.

Mantra the Harmonizing Phrase: *I Love You, Thank You, Please Come Home to Love.*

Surround yourself in the Vesica Piscis.

Rest in the embrace of timelessness.

What Is It? **Practice**

This practice of self-inquiry reveals memories or core beliefs that are triggering pain or disharmony in your life. It's an invitation for your conditioning to rise out of your subconscious into your conscious awareness. The whole point is to welcome the old, habituated pain so that you can offer it your love. Old emotional pain is stagnant, blocked life force, stuck love. The purpose here is to bring that which is stuck in your subconscious to your conscious awareness, so that it can return to its natural flow of love.

It is best done with the curiosity of a child on a scavenger hunt. It's a mystery. Be excited to uncover the golden nugget embedded in the unconscious memory that has arisen and is waiting to be liberated by your loving attention.

What Is It?

Ask yourself what memory is being triggered that's causing you to feel pain or discomfort.

Close your eyes. Let the backs of your eyelids become a movie screen and see what surfaces.

Observe the images or memories that appear on your screen. The scenes may not seem related in any way... just allow them to play out. Your role is to simply observe and stay out of any story.

Mantra *I Love You, Thank You, Please Come Home to Love.*

Whatever It Is Practice

This phrase is used when we don't know what's triggering our pain or discomfort and we just want to address the vibration of its source directly. Without going into further inquiry, we simply offer our presence and love to *whatever it is* that's causing us to feel a certain way.

This practice is very effective with just about anything that causes us discomfort or pain. Some examples might be: physical ailments, mental anxiety, abandonment issues, worries, feelings of unworthiness, lack of abundance.

Whatever It Is...

Say to yourself, Whatever it is that's causing me to feel
_____ (fill in the blank),

I Love You, Thank You, Please Come Home to Love.

Tuning into Your Body's Frequency

Have you ever been asked a question and your body immediately responded with a tightening in your gut, or a tense feeling, or an expansion or opening? Perhaps you have walked into a room full of people and immediately knew you did not want to be there. Yes? Then you have experienced your body's frequency communicating with you. When you are in tune with your body's frequency, you have direct access to knowing what is true or resonant and what is dissonant or inauthentic for you.

Listening to the feeling, the frequency of your body's tuning fork, you hear what the energy in your body is communicating to you. All you have to do is ask your body and it will tell you. Are you feeling relaxed and expanded (resonant) or are you tense and constricted (dissonant)?

Harmonizing Your Body's Frequency Practice

At times, the body's dissonance comes from mental agitation, not from natural response to the present moment. A very quick way to bring harmony to yourself is to simply be aware of and consciously change the frequency in your body. The following practice is to radiate resonance throughout the tuning fork of your body.

Harmonizing Your Body's Frequency

Ask yourself: What am I feeling in my body right now? Resonance or Dissonance?

Place your hand on your heart and bring your awareness to your breath.

Feel the vibration of love in your heart and let it radiate throughout your body, bringing you into resonance with love.

Three Touchstones Practice
(Harmonizing Simplified)

Once you are familiar with the longer version of the Harmonizing Practice, you can easily use the following short version as a quickie:

Three Touchstones

Place your hand on your heart and welcome your feelings.

Mantra *I Love You.*

Surround yourself with the Vesica Piscis.

In Closing

I am one cell in the body of Humanity, whole and complete unto myself. You are one cell in the body of Humanity, whole and complete unto yourself. When we know this, we are free, we are Sovereign.

The purpose of this book is to empower each of us to wake up to the joyful experience of our own unique vibration pulsing through us. Our Sovereignty is felt when the scars and obstructions of our past are being filtered and witnessed by our absolute consciousness. We then feel the flow of pure Love flowing through our free, authentic nature. Life becomes a constant opportunity in all its ups and downs to experience and refine the Love that lives within us.

Our illusion of separation from Love is the root of our suffering. As we reunite our split in consciousness and harmonize our daily life with Love, we heal this experience of separation. We come to know our self as the consciousness of Love.

We give ourselves the great gift that we've always longed for: unconditional loving presence. This is Self-Love. This is Sovereignty.

Appendix

Now they are a circle, and they vibrate together, they pulsate together. Their hearts are no longer separate, their beats are no longer separate, they have become a melody, a harmony... ~ Osho

Deepening

*B*e gentle with yourself. You have just been given a lot of information. Each person will resonate with different parts of it. This is not a practice that you will suddenly internalize. It's a process, and will integrate naturally over time. No need to get stuck in trying to mentally hold on to all of it. The Harmonizing Practice is meant to enhance and complement how you are already living.

To further support you on this journey, the Sovereignty of Love website is available with more information and opportunities to work personally with Alaya, individually or in a group. You can deepen your practice through private Harmonizing sessions, retreats, seminars, and other offerings. Please visit us at:

www.SovereigntyofLove.com

Acknowledgments

$\mathcal{I}$'ve been told that there is a great editor behind every good book. I've been blessed to share this journey hand in hand, side by side with the editor of anyone's dream. Isa Maria, thank you for your relentless love and ruthless commitment and support for this project, for believing in me and for midwifing my fragmented, rambling inspirations into something comprehensible. Thank you for sharing your joy and artistic gift in the exquisite drawings that are spread throughout the book.

I would also like to acknowledge and offer deep gratitude to Michael Shooltz for sharing your presence, wisdom, meticulous editing and kind support from the conception to the birthing of this work, to Shanti Remes for your persistent encouragement to keep going forward and stay focused on this project, and to Kim Murriera for your gentle presence, deep sensitivity, and wise counsel.

I extend eternal love and appreciation to all of my friends, clients, and students, who have continually supported and mirrored my journey.

Gratitude goes to my family for their loving spirits and kind hearts, for being my greatest teachers of love, and for sharing me with this project. Caycee, Shane, Celestine, Alia, Stacey, Dorothy and Steve, I love you.

I applaud Manjari Henderson for her glorious graphics and book cover design, Jamie Saloff for the book's interior design and her unbelievable expertise and generosity in every detail, Paddy Kean and Spencer McDonald for book cover photo and workshop videos. All of them have graciously gone far beyond the call of duty. I am deeply grateful for their brilliance and care.

I bow in humble reverence to the magical island of Kauai and her beauty. She held me in her embrace and shared her love and wisdom as the pages of this book found their coherent expression. Thank You, I Love You.

End Notes

PART ONE: UNIVERSAL PRINCIPLES

Wailua Falls, Kauai, sputnut, www.Bigstock.com

Introduction

Kauai photo of Kuan Yin banana leaf, Candace Freeland,
   www.BluePearlImages.com

Nautilus shell with hands holding, Photosani,
   www.Bigstock.com

Chapter 1

The Physics of Love, Dale Pond, Edgar Cayce, John Keely, Rudolf
   Steiner, Nikola Tesla., p. 16.

Heart Beats, adamson, www.123RF.com

Chapter 2

Tuning fork comics, Isa Maria, www.IsaMaria.com

Water body graphics, Manjari Graphics,
   www.ManjariGraphics.com

Chapter 3

Yin yang symbol, Soleilcl, www.123rf.com

Dual yin yang, Zhuang Mi, www.Dreamstime.com

Water drops ripples, Cammeraydave, www.Dreamstime.com

PART TWO: THE ELEMENTS

Kauai photo of Mt Waialeale, Candace Freeland,
www.BluePearlImages.com

Chapter 5

Mind diagrams, Jamie L. Saloff, www.Saloff.com

Chapter 7

Basic hologram, holograms of consciousness, Manjari Graphics,
www.ManjariGraphics.com

Red rose, Pavlo Vakhrushev, www.Dreamstime.com

Dry rose, Xunin Pan, www.Dreamstime.com

Confused mind, vivid brain, Kts, www.Dreamstime.com

Chapter 8

Toroidal field around heart, Russiangal, www.Dreamstime.com

Chapter 9

Flower of life, Maxim Matisanox, www.123RF. com

Vesica piscis nebulae's, STSci and NASA, www.Hubblesite.org

Partial solar eclipse w/ flares, NASA

End Notes

Partial solar eclipse, Igor Zhorov, www.Dreamstime.com

Human embryo cells, Richard G. Rawlins, Custom Medical
Stock Photo, www.cmsp.com

St. Mary, Radcliffe, Bristol; Robert Cutts, Public Domain,
Generic license, www.Wikipedia.com

Chalice Well Cover, Public Doman, Generic license
Theangryblackwoman, www.en.Wikipedia.com

Sacred heart of Jesus, Zatlectic, www.Bigstock.com

Virgin Mary statue, Kasfeldt7, www.Bigstock.com

Illustrations of meditations, Isa Maria, www.IsaMaria.com

PART THREE: HARMONIZING

Kauai photo of baby beach, Candace Freeland,
www.BluePearlImages.com

Chapter 10

Tuning fork comic, Isa Maria, www.IsaMaria.com

Appendix

Kauai photo of Kalalau, Candace Freeland,
www.BluePearlImages.com

Notes

Water symbol, Konstantin Yuganov, www.Dreamstime.com

About the Author

Alaya DeNoyelles makes her home on the Hawaiian island of Kauai. She practices Five Element Acupuncture and travels to give presentations, workshops, and retreats on the Art of Harmonizing, which she divined from Ho'oponopono, the ancient Hawaiian healing art of reconciliation.

With passionate dedication and soft refinement, she is an expert guide on the journey of awakening to one's authentic, free, sovereign nature. Alaya brings us her talents and wisdom developed through decades of experience as mother, wife, acupuncturist, corporate executive, graphic design artist, teacher and healer.

Notes

Notes

CPSIA information can be obtained at www.ICGtesting.com
Printed in the USA
LVOW05s0414080813

346647LV00004B/225/P